"So I say to you, my friends, that even though we must face the difficulties of today and tomorrow, I still have a dream. It is a dream deeply rooted in the American dream that one day this nation will rise up and live out the true meaning of its creed —we hold these truths to be self-evident, that all men are created equal."

—MARTIN LUTHER KING JR.

THE CIVIL RIGHTS MOVEMENT

BY ROSE VENABLE

The Child's World

COVER PHOTO
Protesters at the March on Washington, August 28, 1963
©Wally McNamee/Corbis

Published in the United States of America by The Child's World®, Inc.
PO Box 326
Chanhassen, MN 55317-0326
800-599-READ
www.childsworld.com

Product Manager Mary Francis-DeMarois/The Creative Spark
Designer Robert E. Bonaker/Graphic Design & Consulting Co.
Editorial Direction Elizabeth Sirimarco
Contributors Mary Berendes, Red Line Editorial, Katherine Stevenson, Ph.D.

The Child's World®, Inc., and Journey to Freedom® are the sole property
and registered trademarks of The Child's World®, Inc.

Library of Congress Cataloging-in-Publication Data
Venable, Rose.
The Civil Rights Movement / by Rose Venable.
p. cm.
Includes bibliographical references and index.
ISBN 1-56766-917-4
1. African Americans—Civil rights—History—20th century—Juvenile literature.
2. Civil rights movements—United States—History—20th century—Juvenile literature.
3. United States—Race relations—Juvenile literature. 4. Racism—United
States—History—20th century—Juvenile literature. [1. African Americans—Civil
rights—History—20th century. 2. Civil rights movements. 3. Race relations.]   I. Title.
E185.61 .T28 2001
323.1'196073'09045—dc21

2001001072

Contents

A Citizen's Rights   6

A Movement for Change   13

The Movement Grows   18

"I Have a Dream"   25

The End of the Civil Rights Movement   31

Timeline   36

Glossary   37

Index   39

Further Information   40

A Citizen's Rights

In the early years of American history, Africans did not come to the United States by choice. They were brought to the New World by slave traders and forced into a life of slavery. For 250 years, slavery was a terrible fact of American life. It was outlawed only when the Civil War ended in 1865. Congress then passed three **amendments** to the **Constitution** guaranteeing the rights of the former slaves. African Americans hoped they would finally enjoy freedom and opportunity as U.S. citizens. Unfortunately, this would not be the case. Even after slavery ended, African Americans faced **discrimination** and **injustice.**

Almost immediately, white people in the southern United States found ways to restrict the rights of African Americans. One of the new Constitutional amendments guaranteed that all black American men could vote. (Women of any race did not win this right until 1920.) Yet white people in the South found ways to break this law. They did not want blacks to have a say in how the government was run. Sometimes they threatened black citizens with violence if they tried to vote. They also passed laws saying that people could register to vote only if they passed a test to prove they could read. In other cases, they said only landowners could vote. Many black people were too poor to buy property. Many had never attended school and could not read. These conditions kept them from being allowed to vote.

Southern states also created **segregation** laws to separate black people from whites. Over the years, more and more of these laws were passed. They affected nearly every part of life for African Americans. Laws said that black people could not eat in the same restaurants, play in the same parks, or drink from the same water fountains as white people. African American children could not go to the same schools as white children. In many cities, black people could not use public transportation.

FOR NEARLY 250 YEARS, SLAVERY WAS A WAY OF LIFE IN THE UNITED STATES. MILLIONS OF PEOPLE, LIKE THE WOMEN SHOWN ABOVE, WORKED AT DIFFICULT JOBS FOR LONG HOURS—WITHOUT EVER RECEIVING PAY FOR THEIR WORK. EVEN AFTER SLAVERY ENDED, AFRICAN AMERICANS WERE NOT TRULY FREE. THEY WERE NOT TREATED AS EQUAL U.S. CITIZENS.

In other places, African Americans had to sit in the backs of streetcars and buses. They also had to give up their seats if there weren't enough seats for all the white people on board.

The northern states had no segregation laws, but that did not mean African Americans were treated fairly. In many places, they were not allowed to buy houses in the same neighborhoods as white people. They could not attend the best schools or hold the best jobs. Throughout the country, black people did not have the same opportunities as whites.

African Americans were never satisfied with their lives as second-class citizens. Even before slavery ended, many courageous people had begun to fight for equality. By the middle of the 20th century, a **movement** had begun in which millions of people worked to win fair treatment for African Americans. Because this movement focused on winning **civil rights,** many history books call it the Civil Rights Movement. Other people call it the Black Freedom Movement.

FOR COLORED ONLY

Bettmann/Corbis

IN THE FIRST HALF OF THE 20TH CENTURY, SIGNS THAT READ "COLORED ONLY" OR "WHITES ONLY" WERE HUNG OVER DRINKING FOUNTAINS, AT RESTAURANTS, ON RESTROOM DOORS, AND IN OTHER PLACES, ESPECIALLY IN THE SOUTHERN STATES. THESE SIGNS CONSTANTLY REMINDED AFRICAN AMERICANS THAT THEY WERE CONSIDERED SECOND-CLASS CITIZENS.

Millions became involved in the Civil Rights Movement—not only adults, but children as well. They held many different kinds of **protests.** In some places, white people became so angry at civil rights protesters that they beat or even killed them.

People have different ideas about when the movement began. Many say it started the moment slavery ended. Others say it began in the early 20th century. Most sources say it began in the 1950s. People also have different ideas about when the movement ended. History books often say it ended when the Voting Rights Act became law in 1965, protecting the voting rights of all Americans. But some people say that the movement never really ended, because African Americans continue to fight for equal rights today.

Long before the Civil Rights Movement gained national attention, African Americans had found ways to fight discrimination. In 1892, for example, a shoemaker named Homer Plessy wanted to do something about segregation laws. He decided to prove that they were **unconstitutional.** To do this, he needed to take a **case** to the U.S. Supreme Court, the highest court in the nation. Plessy boarded a train in New Orleans. Breaking the law, he sat in a car reserved for white people. As Plessy had hoped, he was arrested.

When he went on trial, Plessy argued that segregated railroad cars were unconstitutional. He pointed out that they violated the 14th Amendment to the Constitution, which says that all American citizens have the same rights by law. The judge sent Plessy's case to the Supreme Court. In 1896, the court decided that African Americans could be required to use separate facilities as long as those facilities were equal. This decision became known as the "separate but equal" principle. The results were far from equal, though. Schools, restaurants, and other facilities created for black people were almost always inferior to those reserved for whites.

Some white people showed hatred toward African Americans, especially blacks who spoke out for equality. Some blacks were even **lynched.** Lynching was the most violent form of discrimination African Americans faced. All American citizens accused of a crime have the right to a fair trial to determine whether they are guilty.

Corbis

LONG AFTER HOMER PLESSY TRIED TO END SEGREGATION ON PUBLIC TRANSPORTATION, AFRICAN AMERICANS WERE STILL FORCED TO SIT IN THE BACKS OF BUSES IN MANY PARTS OF THE COUNTRY. DURING THE CIVIL RIGHTS MOVEMENT, MORE AND MORE PEOPLE WOULD CHALLENGE SUCH UNFAIR TREATMENT.

Too often, the right to a fair trial was taken away from black people. Those accused of crimes were not sent to court. Instead, white mobs took justice into their own hands. They assumed blacks were guilty and often murdered them before they ever went to court. Sadly, many of the people these mobs attacked were innocent.

All these forms of injustice inspired more and more African Americans to fight for equality. In the early 1900s, a new group was formed to fight lynching and other forms of **racism.** It was called the National Association for the Advancement of Colored People (often called the NAACP). Over the years, the NAACP became a powerful organization. It encouraged blacks all over the country to join. By the 1930s, its lawyers had begun taking cases to court to challenge discrimination. Many of these challenges were successful.

Corbis

ALTHOUGH SEGREGATION WAS MORE EVIDENT IN THE SOUTH, AFRICAN AMERICANS FACED DISCRIMINATION ALL OVER THE COUNTRY. THEY LIVED IN THE POOREST PARTS OF CITIES AND WORKED AT THE LOWEST-PAYING JOBS. THIS LARGE FAMILY LIVED IN A TINY, RUN-DOWN APARTMENT IN PITTSBURGH, PENNSYLVANIA.

Bettmann/Corbis

SITTING ON THE STEPS OF THE SUPREME COURT BUILDING, A MOTHER TELLS
HER DAUGHTER HOW A COURT DECISION HAS ENDED SEGREGATION IN SCHOOLS.
THIS IMPORTANT VICTORY INSPIRED MANY AFRICAN AMERICANS TO JOIN THE
FIGHT FOR EQUALITY.

A Movement for Change

By the 1950s, the NAACP was fighting its most important court case of all: *Brown versus the Board of Education of Topeka* (Kansas). This case fought segregation in schools. In 1954, the Supreme Court decided that the "separate but equal" law did not apply to schools. It said that segregated schools were illegal according to the U.S. Constitution. Public schools had to be **integrated.** Many consider this decision to be the first major victory of the Civil Rights Movement.

The Supreme Court decision did not immediately end school segregation, however. Many white Southerners fought integration. School employees who helped black children enroll at white schools were fired. White citizens held protests outside schools to which black children had been admitted. Many sent their children to private schools that admitted only whites. In Virginia, one school system closed all its public schools rather than integrate them.

People all over the country read about these events in newspapers. In 1955, a widely publicized tragedy focused even more attention on racial problems in the South. In Mississippi, a group of white men brutally murdered Emmett Till, a 14-year-old black boy. They killed him because he had supposedly whistled at a white woman. The men accused of Till's murder were arrested and went to court. But even though many people had seen them commit the murder, they were found not guilty and set free.

Such terrible stories made people realize that things had to change. African Americans were frustrated that schools were still segregated even after the Supreme Court decision. They realized that the U.S. government could not give them equal rights as quickly as they had hoped. More and more people decided that they had to fight for their own rights.

Library of Congress

A famous bus **boycott** that took place in Montgomery, Alabama, led to an important early victory for the Civil Rights Movement. In Montgomery, blacks were required by law to ride in the back of the bus. On December 1, 1955, Rosa Parks was on her way home after a long day at work. She took a seat in the middle of the bus. Blacks were allowed in the middle seats only if no white person wanted to sit there. When the bus driver ordered Parks to give up her seat to a white man, she quietly refused. She did not become angry or argue. She simply continued to sit in her seat. The bus driver called the police, and Parks was arrested.

Rosa Parks had known this would happen. In fact, she had decided ahead of time that she wanted to challenge this segregation law. She had long been active in the NAACP. From jail, she was allowed to make one phone call. She telephoned her mother, who called E. D. Nixon, president of the local NAACP. He arranged for her to be released so she could go home to await her trial.

ontgomery's African American leaders, including two ministers named Ralph Abernathy and Dr. Martin Luther King Jr., planned a boycott of the buses. They printed 40,000 flyers to tell Montgomery's black community about their idea.

The black residents of Montgomery stopped riding the buses, even though that made life difficult for many of them. A few of Montgomery's black citizens owned cars. They arranged carpools, offering rides to their friends and neighbors and even to strangers. Some people rode bicycles. Most walked wherever they needed to go. Some had to walk long distances to work or to run errands. A few rode mules to their destinations or even arrived on roller skates!

Many white people tried to stop the boycott. The police arrested the carpool drivers. They accused them of picking up hitchhikers, which was against the law. Some African Americans were fired from their jobs for taking part in the boycott. Bombs were thrown into the houses of Dr. King and other NAACP leaders. The protesters were afraid, but they stood firm. The boycott lasted 381 days. It ended on December 20, 1956, when the Supreme Court **ruled** that bus segregation was illegal.

By this time, people around the country knew about the boycott. It made Dr. King famous. As the head of a group called the Southern Christian Leadership Conference (SCLC), King would become the most powerful voice of the Civil Rights Movement. He spoke often about his belief in nonviolent protests such as the boycott. Under no circumstances, said King, should protesters ever resort to violence. Even if they were met with violence, they must remain peaceful. The Montgomery bus boycott had shown that nonviolent protests could work.

The boycott inspired African Americans to fight for their rights in other places, too. Even by the end of 1956, there were still no black students attending school with white children anywhere in the South. When school started in the fall of 1957, nine black students went to enroll at Little Rock Central High School in Little Rock, Arkansas.

Library of Congress

WHEN ROSA PARKS (ABOVE) REFUSED TO GIVE UP HER BUS SEAT TO A WHITE MAN, ONE OF THE MOST FAMOUS PROTESTS OF THE CIVIL RIGHTS MOVEMENT BEGAN.

The governor of Arkansas called out the National Guard to keep the nine students from going to school. President Dwight Eisenhower sent soldiers to take the black children to school. In response, Little Rock officials closed the high school for two years so they would not have to integrate it.

The struggle over integration lasted for years. In 1960, four **federal** marshals took six-year-old Ruby Bridges to enroll at a white school in New Orleans. Parents of the white students withdrew their children from the school. For more than a year, Ruby was the only child in her classroom. Finally, white parents sent their children back to the school.

Library of Congress

WHITE MOTHERS PROTEST OUTSIDE A MARYLAND HIGH SCHOOL AFTER THE FIRST BLACK STUDENTS ENROLLED THERE. MANY SCHOOLS IN THE SOUTH REFUSED TO OBEY THE SUPREME COURT DECISION TO INTEGRATE SCHOOLS.

The Movement Grows

African Americans took great pride in the success of the Montgomery bus boycott. They were hopeful when President Eisenhower sent soldiers to help black students. Inspired by the strides that had been made, more people joined what was now being called the Civil Rights Movement.

Young people in particular became very involved in the movement. Many believed in Martin Luther King's non-violent protests. They used **sit-ins** to fight segregation. They went to restaurants, hotels, parks, and libraries where blacks were not allowed. They walked into these places and sat down. When asked to leave, they quietly refused.

In 1960, one sit-in made national news. Four black college students went into a store in Greensboro, North Carolina. They sat down at its lunch counter. In the past, only white people had been allowed to eat there. The manager of the lunch counter refused to serve them, but the students would not get up. Remaining quiet and calm, they sat there for hours until the restaurant closed.

When they went home, they called friends to tell them about their sit-in. Other people, including white students, decided to join them. Many protesters went to the lunch counter over the next two months. News of their actions spread all over the state and beyond. People began to stage their own sit-ins in other towns and cities.

Crowds of angry white people came to see the sit-ins. They called the protesters names. Some even attacked them, throwing things or hitting them. When the police came, they arrested the protesters, not the people who had attacked them. The protesters remained calm when they were taken to jail. Over time, sit-ins convinced some businesses to take down their "whites only" signs. News reports on sit-ins showed people in the northern states what life was like for black people in the South.

Library of Congress

IN THE 1960S, SIT-INS WERE A COMMON FORM OF PROTEST. DURING THE CIVIL RIGHTS MOVEMENT, MORE THAN 1,700 STUDENTS WERE ARRESTED FOR TAKING PART IN SIT-INS.

Bettmann/Corbis

POLICE ARRESTED THESE TWO
AFRICAN AMERICAN STUDENTS
DURING A SIT-IN AT A TEXAS
DRUGSTORE THAT REFUSED
TO SERVE BLACK CUSTOMERS.

O ver time, young civil rights **activists** organized groups to fight discrimination. They joined a group called the Congress of Racial Equality (CORE). They also formed a new organization called the Student Nonviolent Coordinating Committee (SNCC). Sometimes the SNCC worked with Martin Luther King's organization. But sometimes the groups did not agree. King and other older civil rights leaders often wanted to move more slowly than younger leaders.

In the spring of 1961, college students began the next large-scale protest in the Civil Rights Movement. Members of CORE organized what they called the Freedom Rides. The Supreme Court had decided in December of 1960 that bus and railroad stations could not be segregated. Bus companies that carried passengers from state to state could no longer have separate waiting rooms, bathrooms, and drinking fountains for white and black people. Some white Southerners did not want to obey this decision. To show the public that discrimination against blacks still occurred, black and white CORE activists rode two buses from Washington, D.C., to New Orleans.

The first bus trip was difficult for the Freedom Riders. At first, people just glared or yelled at them. But two days into the trip, one bus stopped in Rockhill, South Carolina. When a young black Freedom Rider tried to go into the "whites only" waiting room, he was beaten. A man and woman who came to his defense were attacked as well.

Even though the Riders faced violence and hatred, they continued to organize protests. In Anniston, Alabama, a mob attacked a bus carrying Freedom Riders. They slashed its tires when it pulled into the station. The driver decided not to stop and kept driving. But angry white people piled into cars and followed the bus out of town. When all of its tires went flat, it had to pull to the side of the road. The mob surrounded the bus, smashing its windows. Someone threw a bomb, and the bus caught fire. When state police arrived, they took the Freedom Riders to the hospital.

Another mob attacked Freedom Riders in Birmingham, Alabama. Some of the Riders were badly hurt. One had to have 53 stitches to heal cuts on his face.

The same mob even attacked news reporters who came to cover the Freedom Rides. The reporters told the public about the Freedom Riders and about their own experiences. Americans were amazed that the Freedom Riders were willing to face such danger to end discrimination.

For a time, the Freedom Rides stopped. No bus driver would agree to carry the Riders. But the Rides started again after President John F. Kennedy made arrangements for state police to protect the Riders. This protection could not keep the Riders from being arrested, though. Freedom Riders were arrested in Mississippi on charges of disturbing the peace. They went to prison for months.

Martin Luther King's organization, the SCLC, started a new project in the spring of 1963. The SCLC began holding marches and sit-ins in Birmingham, Alabama. On May 2, thousands of schoolchildren took part in one especially large march. Bull Connor, head of the Birmingham police, sent officers to arrest the protesters. About 600 children were sent to jail.

Bettmann/Corbis

ALTHOUGH MOST PEOPLE INVOLVED IN THE CIVIL RIGHTS MOVEMENT BELIEVED IN PEACEFUL PROTESTS, POLICE AND OTHER LAW ENFORCEMENT OFFICIALS OFTEN ATTACKED THEM. IN MAY OF 1963, POLICE SPRAYED FIRE HOSES AT PROTESTERS DURING A DEMONSTRATION IN BIRMINGHAM, ALABAMA.

The next day, another march took place. This time, the Birmingham police used high-powered fire hoses to attack the marchers. The force of the water was so strong, it knocked grown men off their feet. Children struck by the water were sent tumbling down the street. When people continued to march, the police brought out dogs and ordered them to attack the marchers—including children.

News cameras captured these terrible events. That night, people all over the world saw what was going on, and they were outraged. More and more civil rights activists came to Birmingham to show their support for the people there. News reporters also came in greater numbers. White storeowners worried because the demonstrations were making them lose business. They asked the city government to change its segregation laws. Birmingham officials agreed. But violence continued in Birmingham as members of a hate group, the **Ku Klux Klan,** bombed black people's homes and churches. Even so, the events in Birmingham were a huge victory. What happened there gained nationwide support for the Civil Rights Movement.

In the meantime, civil rights efforts had continued elsewhere. In 1962, a man named James Meredith applied for admission to law school at the University of Mississippi. When school officials refused to let him attend, he took the university to court. The Supreme Court ruled that he must be admitted. When the governor of the state tried to prevent Meredith from attending, President Kennedy sent federal marshals to take him to classes. A **riot** broke out when white students began to harass the marshals. By the time it ended, two people had been killed and about 375 people injured.

A year later, Alabama governor George Wallace tried to prevent African American students from attending the University of Alabama. President Kennedy sent the National Guard to help the students. In a speech, Wallace said that the federal government was wrong to fight for African Americans' civil rights. In response, an angry President Kennedy gave a televised speech in which he called segregation morally wrong. Now even the nation's president was speaking out against discrimination.

Flip Schulke/Corbis

ON AUGUST 28, 1963, ABOUT 250,000 PROTEST-
ERS GATHERED AROUND THE LINCOLN MEMORIAL
DURING THE MARCH ON WASHINGTON —ONE OF
THE MOST SIGNIFICANT EVENTS OF THE CIVIL
RIGHTS MOVEMENT.

"I Have a Dream"

In a 1963 speech, President Kennedy promised to push a civil rights **bill** through Congress. He said he would introduce a bill making it illegal to discriminate against anyone because of race. Civil rights leaders considered this a huge victory. But the very night Kennedy delivered his speech, activist Medgar Evers was killed in Jackson, Mississippi.

Evers was a civil rights leader who had organized sit-ins and other protests. He also had begun helping blacks register to vote. A Ku Klux Klan member, Byron De La Beckwith, murdered Evers for his commitment to the movement. Beckwith was arrested for the crime but was found not guilty in two separate trials. For years Evers's wife, Myrlie, kept trying to put her husband's murderer behind bars. She finally succeeded 30 years after Evers's death. In 1994, Beckwith was found guilty of murdering Medgar Evers and sentenced to life in prison.

In 1963, Evers's death made it clear that the Civil Rights Movement still had much to accomplish. To convince Congress to pass President Kennedy's bill, civil rights leaders organized the March on Washington. This demonstration was held on August 28, 1963. Many organizations cooperated to make the March happen. About 250,000 people of all races and from all over the nation came to show their support.

The greatest moment of this inspiring day took place when Martin Luther King stepped up to speak to the crowd. He delivered a stirring speech in which he summed up his hopes for America. "I have a dream," proclaimed Dr. King, "my four little children will one day live in a nation where they will not be judged by the color of their skin but by the content of their character. I have a dream today!" King's "I Have a Dream" speech became the most famous of his career. His words came to symbolize the noblest goals of the movement.

Flip Schulke/Corbis

The March on Washington inspired people all over the country. Those who took part returned home and continued their efforts. People all over the country were committed to making life better for African Americans. Sadly, some white people were still committed to stopping them.

In September of 1963, one of the greatest tragedies of the Civil Rights Movement took place. A bomb was planted at a black church in Birmingham, Alabama. Four little girls attending Sunday school were killed. Americans again expressed outrage and sorrow. And yet some members of Congress still said they wouldn't vote for a civil rights law.

WHEN MARTIN LUTHER KING JR. GAVE HIS SPEECH AT THE MARCH ON WASHINGTON, HIS WORDS MOVED EVERYONE. "THERE WILL BE NEITHER REST NOR TRANQUILITY IN AMERICA," SAID KING, "UNTIL THE NEGRO IS GRANTED HIS CITIZENSHIP RIGHTS. THE WHIRLWINDS OF REVOLT WILL CONTINUE TO SHAKE THE FOUNDATIONS OF OUR NATION UNTIL THE BRIGHT DAY OF JUSTICE EMERGES."

On November 22, 1963, President John Kennedy was **assassinated.** Vice President Lyndon Johnson became the new president. At first, civil rights leaders worried that Kennedy's law would never become reality. But Johnson shared the dream of equality. He followed in Kennedy's footsteps and pushed Congress to pass the Civil Rights Act of 1964. This law outlawed segregation in all public places. It allowed the U.S. government to enforce integration in schools. It also allowed the government to withhold funds from public schools that refused to integrate. When Johnson signed the bill into law on July 2, it was a huge victory for the Civil Rights Movement. The protesters who had fought so hard for justice and equality had, in fact, changed America.

This important law was a step in the right direction. But members of the movement were still fighting another form of discrimination: restriction of voting rights. Civil rights leaders knew that if more African Americans voted, they would have more say in the government. They wanted to register more African Americans to vote.

Bettmann/Corbis

ON JULY 2, 1964, PRESIDENT LYNDON JOHNSON SIGNED THE CIVIL RIGHTS ACT INTO LAW. HERE HE SHAKES HANDS WITH MARTIN LUTHER KING AND GIVES HIM THE PEN USED FOR SIGNING THE ACT.

In 1963, voter registration drives had begun in Mississippi, Alabama, and Georgia. The following year, members of the SNCC started what they called Freedom Schools. The Freedom Schools taught blacks to read and write so they could pass the tests required to vote.

In the summer of 1964, student volunteers from the North traveled to Mississippi. Many of these young people were white. They planned to run a massive voter registration drive called "Freedom Summer." Sadly, more violence took place. Three of these activists disappeared and were later found dead. They had been kidnapped and murdered for helping black people register to vote.

Civil rights leaders needed to do more to protect the right to vote. In March of 1965, they held a huge protest in Selma, Alabama. Thousands of African Americans went to the Selma courthouse, asking to take the voter registration test. The sheriff had them arrested. His deputies beat some of the protesters. Refusing to give up, the protesters planned a march to Montgomery,

Alabama's capital, on March 7. Police officers on horseback clubbed and beat the protesters. Films of police attacking the protesters appeared on televisions all over the country. Americans were horrified at the events that took place on "Bloody Sunday."

The next day, protesters returned to continue the march. But police again arrived to stop them. That night, one minister who joined the protest was badly beaten. He later died from his wounds. Americans from across the country, white and black, demanded that another law be passed to protect the voting rights of all U.S. citizens. Right away, President Johnson vowed to make Congress pass a voting-rights law.

Johnson kept his promise. On March 15, eight days after "Bloody Sunday," he introduced the bill to Congress. On March 20, Martin Luther King organized another march to bring attention to Johnson's bill. He led marchers on a four-day journey from Selma to Montgomery. This time, federal troops stood by to protect them.

As the protesters marched, more and more people joined them. By the time they reached the capitol building in Montgomery, the marchers were 25,000 strong. All were demanding protection of the right to vote.

That summer, on August 6, Congress passed the Voting Rights Act of 1965. This law required the national government to supervise all voter registration in the South. Between 1965 and 1968, one million African Americans in the South voted for the first time.

Bettmann/Corbis

ON MARCH 20, 1965, MARTIN LUTHER KING LED THOUSANDS OF CIVIL RIGHTS PROTESTERS ON A 50-MILE MARCH FROM SELMA, ALABAMA, TO THE STATE CAPITAL OF MONTGOMERY. THEY HOPED TO CALL ATTENTION TO THE VOTING RIGHTS ACT.

Corbis

THREE BOYS PLAY BASEBALL IN THE ALLEY OF A WASHINGTON, D.C., SLUM. AFTER THE VOTING RIGHTS ACT OF 1965 TOOK EFFECT, MARTIN LUTHER KING BEGAN TO TALK ABOUT A NEW GOAL FOR THE CIVIL RIGHTS MOVEMENT: TO HELP AFRICAN AMERICANS BEYOND THE SOUTH ESCAPE POVERTY AND INNER-CITY SLUMS.

The End of the Civil Rights Movement

After blacks began to vote in the South, Martin Luther King talked about new goals for the Civil Rights Movement. The movement had focused on change in the South and had accomplished great things. But African Americans in the North felt that nothing had been done to help them. They had never faced segregation laws. Few had experienced difficulty trying to vote. Yet many lived in inner-city slums, trapped by poverty. King wanted to help blacks in northern states fight racism as well.

African Americans throughout the nation were still locked out of the best schools, the best neighborhoods, and the best jobs. They had no access to the opportunities white Americans enjoyed. A government committee created by President Johnson described the United States as "a nation moving towards two societies—one black, one white, separate but unequal." Civil rights protests began in the North, but change was slow to come.

Some young blacks questioned King's goals and his methods. They did not share his belief that the United States would be fully integrated one day. They also didn't believe that civil rights workers should refuse to fight back if attacked. Instead, they supported the ideas of another African American leader, Malcolm X. For years, Malcolm X had said that blacks should fight back. He also said that blacks should not work for integration. Instead, he believed the races should remain separate, but that blacks should fight to gain power. Malcolm X was assassinated in February of 1965, but his views became increasingly popular among activists frustrated by slow progress.

In the summer of 1965, just five days after President Johnson signed the Voting Rights Act, race riots broke out in the city of Los Angeles, California.

Over the next six days, 50,000 African Americans took to the streets, stealing from shops, setting fire to white-owned businesses, and shooting law officers. By the end of the riots, 34 people had been killed, 900 hurt, and 4,000 arrested. Riots followed in Chicago and in Springfield, Massachusetts. Unfortunately, more race riots took place the following summer.

Corbis

IN THE SUMMER OF 1965, RACE RIOTS BROKE OUT IN THE WATTS SECTION OF LOS ANGELES. HERE A GROUP OF PEOPLE SURVEY THE DAMAGE AFTER A NIGHT OF VIOLENCE.

These were troubled times. Civil rights leaders disagreed on what to do. More and more blacks began to say they no longer believed in Martin Luther King's policy of nonviolence.

On April 4, 1968, Martin Luther King was assassinated in Memphis, Tennessee. Americans of all races mourned his death. Afterward, blacks disagreed even more about how to fight for equality. Young blacks had begun to talk about a new Black Power movement. Those involved in it were angry that racism still existed even after the tremendous efforts of civil rights workers in the 1950s and 1960s.

Black Power supporters agreed with Malcolm X's belief that blacks needed to be completely independent from whites. Some formed a new group called the Black Panther Party.

Library of Congress

MALCOLM X (ABOVE) HAD VERY DIFFERENT IDEAS FROM THOSE OF MARTIN LUTHER KING. HE BELIEVED THAT BLACKS MIGHT HAVE TO USE VIOLENCE TO FIGHT DISCRIMINATION. HIS IDEAS BECAME INCREASINGLY POPULAR WITH AFRICAN AMERICANS WHO WERE FRUSTRATED BY HOW SLOWLY CHANGE WAS TAKING PLACE.

Black Panther members believed that black protesters should defend themselves when demonstrations became violent—even if that meant using violence themselves. Some Black Panthers were killed in fights with police officers. Others went to prison. By the late 1960s, many people said the Civil Rights Movement had ended, but groups like the Black Panthers continued to fight for equality, justice, and opportunity.

African Americans had gained important victories during the Civil Rights Movement. Legal segregation no longer existed. Blacks in the South could now vote. African American leaders began to win elections and take part in local, state, and national government. Sadly, many important leaders in the movement had been killed, including Medger Evers, Malcolm X, and Martin Luther King Jr. And although much had been gained, there was still much work to be done.

Today Americans express great pride in the achievements of the Civil Rights Movement. Many say, however, that discrimination still keeps the United States from being a land truly dedicated to freedom. In the early 21st century, people continue to fight racism and discrimination, seeking justice and opportunity for all.

Bettmann/Corbis

A GROUP OF AFRICAN AMERICANS GIVE THE BLACK POWER SALUTE, RAISING THEIR FISTS IN THE AIR. SUPPORTERS OF THE BLACK POWER MOVEMENT FOCUSED NOT ON INTEGRATION INTO WHITE AMERICA, BUT ON GIVING BLACKS THE MEANS TO BE INDEPENDENT AND SUCCESSFUL WITHIN THEIR OWN COMMUNITIES.

Bettmann/Corbis

THE ACHIEVEMENTS OF THE CIVIL RIGHTS MOVEMENT—AND THE COURAGE OF THOSE WHO PARTICIPATED IN IT—CONTINUE TO INSPIRE AMERICANS TODAY.

Timeline

1896	In the court case *Plessy versus Ferguson*, the Supreme Court rules that segregation is legal as long as blacks have access to equal facilities. This ruling becomes known as the "separate but equal" principle.
1909	The National Association for the Advancement of Colored People (NAACP) is founded.
1954	The NAACP's lawyers go to trial in an important case, *Brown versus the Board of Education of Topeka* (Kansas). At the end of the trial, the Supreme Court rules that public schools cannot be segregated.
1955	In August, 14-year-old Emmett Till is murdered in Mississippi by a group of white men.
	In December, Rosa Parks is arrested in Montgomery, Alabama, after refusing to give up her bus seat to a white man. Black community leaders, including Martin Luther King Jr. and Ralph Abernathy, plan a boycott to protest segregation on buses.
1956	The Supreme Court rules that bus segregation is illegal. The Montgomery bus boycott ends on December 20 after 381 days.
1957	Black students are barred from enrolling at a public high school in Little Rock, Arkansas. After the federal government says they must be allowed to enroll, Little Rock closes the school rather than admit blacks.
	Martin Luther King Jr. founds a new civil rights organization, the Southern Christian Leadership Conference (SCLC).
1960	A famous sit-in takes place in North Carolina when four black college students sit down at a lunch counter.
1961	Young black and white activists ride buses from Washington, D.C., to New Orleans. Along the

way, they protest the fact that bus stations are still segregated, even though the Supreme Court has declared this against the law. These protests, known as the Freedom Rides, gain national attention.

1962	James Meredith tries to enroll at the University of Mississippi Law School. After the Supreme Court declares that he must be admitted, a riot takes place in which two people die and many more are hurt.
1963	Civil rights leaders begin voter registration drives in the South.
	On June 12, President John F. Kennedy gives a speech in which he promises to make Congress pass a civil rights bill. That same night, civil rights activist Medgar Evers is murdered.
	The March on Washington takes place on August 28. More than 250,000 people attend to show their support for civil rights laws.
	In September, four little girls are killed in a church bombing in Birmingham, Alabama.
	In November, President Kennedy is assassinated.
1964	Student volunteers travel to the South to organize voter registration drives. Three volunteers are kidnapped and murdered.
	With the support of President Lyndon Baines Johnson, the Civil Rights Act becomes law on July 2.
1965	Police attack civil rights protesters at a march in Selma, Alabama.
	President Johnson signs the Voting Rights Act into law on August 6, protecting the right of all U.S. citizens to vote.
1968	The Black Power movement begins. Martin Luther King is assassinated on April 4.

Glossary

activists (AK-tiv-ists)
Activists are people who take strong action to support a view or belief. Civil rights activists worked to achieve better treatment for African Americans.

amendments (uh-MEND-ments)
Amendments are changes made to a law or an official document. An amendment to the U.S. Constitution ended slavery.

assassinated (uh-SASS-ih-nayt-ed)
When an important or famous person has been murdered, he or she has been assassinated. Many civil rights leaders were assassinated.

bill (BILL)
A bill is an idea or plan for a new law that is presented to a group of lawmakers. President Kennedy promised to push Congress to pass a civil rights bill.

boycott (BOY-kot)
A boycott is a protest in which people stop using a certain product or service. A bus boycott helped end segregation on public buses in Montgomery, Alabama.

case (KAYSS)
A case is a matter for a court of law to decide. To fight discrimination, the NAACP took many cases to court.

civil rights (SIV-il RYTZ)
Civil rights are a person's rights to freedom and equal treatment. The Civil Rights Movement focused on winning equal treatment for African Americans.

Constitution (kon-stih-TOO-shun)
The United States Constitution is the document that lays out how the nation will be governed. Three additions to the Constitution guaranteed the rights of former slaves.

discrimination (dis-krim-ih-NAY-shun)
Discrimination is the unfair treatment of people simply because they are different. Even after slavery ended, African Americans struggled against discrimination.

federal (FED-er-ull)
Federal means having to do with the nation's central government rather than a state or local government. In 1960, four federal marshals took Ruby Bridges to enroll at a white school.

injustice (in-JUSS-tiss)
Injustice is something that is unfair or wrong. People who are denied equal rights are victims of injustice.

integrated (IN-teh-gray-ted)
If something is integrated, all people can use it equally. In 1954, the Supreme Court declared that all public schools must be integrated.

Glossary

Ku Klux Klan (KOO KLUKS KLAN)
The Ku Klux Klan is a hate group that believes white people of certain religions are better than other people. The Ku Klux Klan has committed many acts of violence against African Americans, as well as against other people.

lynched (LINCHD)
When a person is lynched, they are put to death—often by hanging—by a mob. Instead of receiving a fair trial, some black people in the South were lynched for crimes they did not commit.

movement (MOOV-ment)
A movement is an organized effort to achieve a certain goal. The Civil Rights Movement was the struggle for equal rights for African Americans in the United States during the 1950s and 1960s.

protests (PROH-tests)
Protests are public statements or gatherings in which people speak out to say something is wrong. Activists held many kinds of protests during the Civil Rights Movement.

racism (RAY-sih-zim)
Racism is a negative feeling or opinion about people because of their race. The NAACP was formed to fight lynching and other forms of racism.

riot (RY-ut)
A riot is a violent public disturbance by a large group of people. Five days after the Voting Rights Act was signed, riots broke out in Los Angeles.

ruled (ROOLD)
When a court has ruled on a case, it has made a decision. In 1954, all nine judges on the Supreme Court ruled to end segregation in public schools.

segregation (seh-greh-GAY-shun)
Segregation is the practice of using laws to keep people apart. Segregation laws separated blacks and whites in the South for many years.

sit-ins (SIT-inz)
A sit-in is a kind of protest in which people sit down and refuse to leave. During the Civil Rights Movement, sit-ins helped end segregation in restaurants.

unconstitutional (un-kon-stih-TOO-shun-ul)
If something is unconstitutional, it is not allowed by the U.S. Constitution. Homer Plessy wanted to prove that segregation laws were unconstitutional.

Index

Abernathy, Ralph, 15, 36
Africans, 6
Alabama, 23, 28
Anniston, Alabama, 21

Birmingham, Alabama, 21-23, 26, 36
Birmingham church bombing, 26, 36
Black Freedom Movement, 8
Black Panther Party, 33, 36
Black Power movement, 33, 36
"Bloody Sunday," 28
boycotts, 14. *See also* Montgomery bus boycott
Bridges, Ruby, 17
Brown versus the Board of Education of Topeka (Kansas), 13, 36

Chicago, 32
citizenship, 6, 7
civil rights, 8, 9, 11, 23
Civil Rights Act of 1964, 25, 26, 27, 36
Civil Rights Movement, 8, 10, 25
    arrests of participants, 14, 19, 20, 21, 22
    beginning of, 9
    end of, 9, 31-33
    the media and, 13, 18, 21, 23, 28
    poverty and, 30, 31
    victories of, 13, 15, 18, 24, 27, 29, 34
Civil War, 6, 36
Congress of Racial Equality (CORE), 20
Congress, U. S., 6, 25, 26, 27, 28
Connor, Bull, 21
Constitution, U. S., 6, 13

De La Beckwith, Byron, 25
discrimination, 6, 9, 11, 21, 23, 25, 34. *See also* racism, segregation

Eisenhower, Dwight D., 17, 18
equality, equal rights, 8, 9, 10, 12, 13, 27, 33
Evers, Medgar, 25, 34, 36
Evers, Myrlie, 25

15th Amendment, 36
14th Amendment, 9, 36
Freedom Rides, 20-21, 36
Freedom Schools, 28
"Freedom Summer," 28

Georgia, 28
Greensboro, North Carolina, 18, 36

"I Have a Dream" speech, 25, 26
integration, 13, 17, 27, 31, 33

Jackson, Mississippi, 25
Johnson, Lyndon B., 27, 28, 31, 36

Kennedy, John F., 21, 23, 25, 27, 36
King, Dr. Martin Luther Jr., 15, 18, 20, 21, 25-26, 27, 28-29, 30-31, 32, 33, 34, 36
Ku Klux Klan, 25

Lincoln Memorial, 24, 25
Little Rock, Arkansas, 15, 17, 36

Little Rock Central High School, 15
Los Angeles (Watts), 31-32
lynching, 9, 11

Malcolm X, 31, 33, 34
the March on Washington, 24, 25-26, 36
Maryland, 17
Memphis, Tennessee, 33
Meredith, James, 23, 36
Mississippi, 13, 21, 28, 36
Montgomery, Alabama, 14-15, 28, 29, 36
Montgomery bus boycott, 14-15, 16, 17, 18, 36

National Association for the Advancement of Colored People (NAACP), 11, 13, 14, 15, 36
National Guard, 17, 23
New Orleans, 9, 17, 20, 36
Nixon, E. D., 14-15
nonviolence, 15, 18, 33
Northern states, the North, 8, 28, 31

Parks, Rosa, 14-15, 16, 36
Pittsburgh, Pennsylvania, 11
Plessy, Homer, 9, 10
Plessy versus Ferguson, 36
protests, 9, 13, 16, 19, 25, 31. *See also* boycotts, Montgomery Bus Boycott, sit-ins

race riots, 31-33
racism, 11, 31, 33, 34. *See also* discrimination, segregation
Rockhill, South Carolina, 21

segregation, 6, 7, 9-12, 13-15, 18, 20, 23, 27, 34
    See also discrimination, racism
Selma, Alabama, 28, 29, 36
"separate but equal," 9, 13
sit-ins, 18, 19, 20, 21, 25
slavery, 6, 7, 9
Southern Christian Leadership Conference (SCLC), 15, 21, 36
Southern states, the South, 6, 11, 13, 15, 17, 18, 29, 30, 34
Springfield, Massachusetts, 32
Student Nonviolent Coordinating Committee (SNCC), 20, 28
Supreme Court, U. S., 9, 12, 13, 15, 17, 20, 23, 36

Texas, 20
13th Amendment, 36
Till, Emmett, 13, 14, 36

United States, 6, 7, 31, 34
University of Alabama, 23
University of Mississippi, 23, 36

violence, 6, 9, 14, 15, 18, 21, 22, 23, 25, 28, 33
Virginia, 13
voter registration drives, 28
voting rights, 6, 25, 27-30, 34
Voting Rights Act of 1965, 9, 28, 29, 30, 31, 36

Wallace, George, 23
Washington, D. C., 20, 30, 36

Further Information

Books and Magazines

Crushshon, Theresa. *Malcolm X.* Chanhassen, MN: The Child's World, 2002.

Darby, Jean. *Martin Luther King.* Minneapolis, MN: Lerner Publications, 1990.

King, Casey, et al. *Oh Freedom! Kids Talk about the Civil Rights Movement with the People Who Made It Happen.* New York: Knopf, 1997.

Summer, L. S. *The March on Washington.* Chanhassen, MN: The Child's World, 2001.

Turck, Mary. *The Civil Rights Movement for Kids: A History with 21 Activities.* Chicago: Chicago Review Press, 2000.

Web Sites

Visit a Civil Rights timeline posted by students at Western Michigan University:
http://www.wmich.edu/politics/mlk

Visit the Web site of the National Civil Rights Museum:
http://www.mecca.org/~crights/

Visit a site about Martin Luther King that includes links to other sites of interest:
http://martinlutherking.8m.com/

Learn more about Rosa Parks and the Montgomery bus boycott:
http://www.holidays.net/mlk/rosa.htm

Learn more about *Brown versus the Board of Education of Topeka* (Kansas):
http://brownvboard.org

Learn more about Malcolm X:
http://www.malcolm-x.org